The Painted Rocks

Written by
Ruth Alter

Designed & Illustrated by
Sandra Shaw

DEDICATION

This book is dedicated
to the children of
San Pasqual Reservation
in the hope that their futures
may reflect their past
and
to the memory of MHL

Funds for this printing of the book were made possible through a grant from the San Pasqual Band of Mission Indians. The original printing was funded by a grant from the State of California Department of Parks and Recreation and the City of San Diego's San Dieguito River Valley Trust Fund. All proceeds will be used to further the protection, interpretation, and understanding of the Piedras Pintadas site, a site which serves as a physical link to the past for contemporary Kumeyaay and as a source of wonderment for all people.

ACKNOWLEDGMENTS

The Painted Rocks is the product of many minds. Special thanks to Johnny Contreras and Jim and Olga Quisquis of San Pasqual Reservation for their kindness and for unselfishly sharing their heritage, and to G. Timothy Gross, Michael Baksh, Ken Hedges, and Florence Shipek for their valuable comments and insights about Kumeyaay culture.

Back cover photo courtesy of Steven Freers.

TABLE OF CONTENTS

SPECIAL TOPICS

ILLUSTRATIONS

**Words to be found in the Glossary are italicized in the story and Special Topics*

1

A NOT-SO-NORMAL AFTERNOON

The afternoon Cassie McKenzie discovered there was something special just beyond her backyard started like any normal afternoon. She came home from school at two o'clock, put her books down, said "hello" to her mother, ate a cookie, and took her dog, Heidi, for a walk. Normal, normal, normal.

Cassie did the same thing every day. She went out the same back door, out the same backgate, and down the same trail into the big open area behind her house. Sometimes she wondered if Heidi ever got as tired of seeing the same things every day as she did!

Not that she didn't like where she lived—she did. Their house had two stories and her bedroom overlooked the open area. Sometimes on summer nights when her bedroom windows were open, she could hear the coyotes singing to the moon, and she liked to watch the rain falling against the hillsides in the winter. Even though it was same-old, same-old, Cassie loved the wildness just beyond her neighborhood. She felt it belonged to her, just the way their house did.

When they first moved into the house, Cassie had been too small to wander down the trail by herself, of course. She had gone with her mother and father, and Jeffrey, her older brother. Heidi was just a puppy then. Now Heidi was getting old. She couldn't go as fast as she used to and she was decidedly grumpier, but she seemed to look forward to the daily walk anyway.

This afternoon, the two took their time. Cassie always liked the view from this part of the trail. Below her was Lake Hodges and sometimes she could see small boats on the water. There weren't any boats there today. The view was ringed by very steep hills and mountains with towering boulders on their slopes. The boulders seemed to be standing guard, like silent soldiers at their posts. They made Cassie feel safe and sheltered.

Cassie and Heidi always stayed right on the trail, because, for one thing, the open area was overgrown with weeds and tall grass and their stickers got caught in Heidi's fur, and for another, snakes hid in the brush and in the rocks on the hillsides all around them. Cassie didn't like snakes; she didn't think Heidi did either!

As they came down the trail, the sound of voices and laughter floated up. At the trail bottom the open space widened, and off to one side in front of her, Cassie saw a group of people. Most of them were boys, maybe just a few years older than she was, but there were grownups there, too. She watched them for a while. They were dressed in old-looking clothes and some of them had cotton work gloves like her mother sometimes wore when she gardened. There was lots of talking going on. They looked like they were getting ready for something to begin.

One man seemed to be in charge. He was passing out dark green plastic trash bags to everyone. When he saw Cassie, he motioned to

PIEDRAS PINTADAS

Piedras Pintadas is a real archaeological site. It is located in Rancho Bernardo, a community in north central San Diego County, California. The site is being protected as part of an open space park that has been created along the San Dieguito River.

KUMEYAAY WORDS

mano	**hepechaa**
metate	**'ehpii**
mortar	**'ehmuu**
bow	**'aatim**
arrow	**'epal**
arrowhead	**pawiiy**
olla	**'aaskay**
sandals	**hemenyaaw**
throwing stick	**hempuu**
carrying net	**hallepuu**
cradleboard	**'uukwill**
baby	**hekwaal**
bird	**'aashaa**

her. "Would you like to help us?," he called out.

Cassie looked at the man as she walked toward him. He was older than she was, but definitely younger than her mother or father. He looked younger than the other adults there, too. His hair was very black and shiny, and it was pulled back into a long straight ponytail. When the man smiled, his teeth were even and white. He had dark, sparkly eyes. There was something very nice about him. She liked him right away. Even grumpy Heidi wagged her tail.

"Hi," the man said in a quiet, steady voice. "I'm Tom Quahan."

"I'm Cassie McKenzie, and this is Heidi," Cassie replied.

"Nice to meet you, Cassie," Tom said. "Do you live around here?"

When she told him she did and pointed up to her house, Tom said, "We're having a work party today to clean up Piedras Pintadas. These scouts and their folks have made this their service project and we're just about to get started. It's our first work party. We're going to pick up as much trash as we can this afternoon and we can use all the hands we can get, so if you want to help, we could use you. When we're done, I'm going to talk about the area. You could stay for that, too, if you'd like."

Cassie had never heard the name Piedras Pintadas used before. But helping Tom sounded like fun even though she knew she'd probably have to get off the trail and walk around in the brush. "Oh well," she told herself, "I'll just be careful."

To Tom she said, "O.K., thanks! I'm going to take Heidi home and tell my mom where I am, then I'll be right back!"

She practically dragged poor Heidi up the trail. As she came back down to join Tom and the others, Cassie McKenzie had a suspicion that this wasn't going to be such a normal afternoon after all!

butterfly	**mes-haalyap**	hello	**haawka**
agave	**'emally**	house	**'ewaa**
child	**'elymaam**	lizard	**haakwal**
cloud	**'ekwiiy**	man	**'iikwich**
coyote	**hattepaa**	woman	**siny**
deer	**'ekwak**		
friend	**unyeway**		

The Kumeyaay told many different stories to their children so they would know about the world and how to behave in it. This is a retelling of part of the Kumeyaay origin story told to a writer named Mellicent Lee, about 1920.

HOW OLDER BROTHER CREATED THE WORLD

A long time ago when the world was covered with water, two brothers lived deep down in the earth. Each had a special animal to keep him company—the older brother had a badger and the younger brother had a soft, yellow-haired desert kit fox. The older brother wanted the fox, but the younger brother wouldn't give it to him.

2

TOM'S TALK

By the time Cassie rejoined the group, everyone was busy picking up bottles and cans and paper from the ground. Cassie had never noticed before just how much litter and trash had accumulated. She looked around her and doubted whether it all could be picked up in a single afternoon or even in four afternoons, for that matter. But it pleased to her to see how much better everything looked when it was clean. She wondered why people couldn't pick up after themselves.

They worked steadily. Every so often someone would fill a trash bag and go to Tom for another. A few of the parents sat and sorted through the trash, setting aside the glass, metal, paper, and plastic for recycling. While Cassie worked, she was aware of the low hum people make sometimes when they're working together—a sort of soft, peaceful, soothing sound that was very pleasant. She was also aware of the sweet, earthy smell of the plants all around them. A little breeze came up and carried the smell everywhere Cassie went.

After the group had worked for over an hour, Tom called for everyone to stop. He asked them to gather up the trash bags and come sit down. He motioned to a cleared place near some rocks.

With the trash bags collected, the group assembled in the place Tom had indicated. The lake shimmered below them in the afternoon sunlight. For a minute or two, people continued to talk together in low voices, but they stopped when Tom began to speak.

" You've done a good job here, today," he said. "Your effort is appreciated very much. I know there's a lot more work to be done, but we made a big start. Each time we come back, it will be a little easier. This is a very special place for me and I hope it will be for you, too. Thank you for taking on this project."

Then, beginning his introduction in a quiet, clear voice, he said, "My name is Tom Quahan. I hope to know all your names before our project is over. I'm a Kumeyaay Indian and I'm a member of the San Pasqual Band. Our reservation is north of here, in Valley Center. I didn't grow up on the reservation, but I live there now."

Grinning he added, "My mom and dad are city people, so I grew up in town and went to school there, but my grandparents and my uncles and their families live on the reservation and we always were there visiting and helping with the work when I was young.

"In college I studied art, and afterwards I decided to start a business designing and crafting furniture. My grandfather helped me set up a little workshop next to his house, so that's how I came back to the reservation."

Tom paused, "What I'm going to tell you comes partly from what my family and our elders have taught me, partly from what I've learned from people who study ***archaeology*** and ***anthropology***, and partly from what I've observed on my own. Something important I've learned is that sometimes

Origin Story (continued)

One day Older Brother suggested they go up to the top of world to see what was there. Clutching his badger, he took a deep breath, closed his eyes, and up through the green water he went. When he reached the top and looked around, all he saw was water everywhere. Younger Brother wanted to see the top of the world too. "How do I get through the water?" he called. And Older Brother told him, "You open your eyes and swim to the top. But you will need to use your hands, so I will hold your fox for you."

Younger Brother passed his fox to his brother, opened his eyes and swam upward. When he reached the top, the green water had made him blind. He asked for his fox, but Older Brother handed him the badger instead.

people have very different ideas about the same thing and sometimes no one knows for sure about the way some things happened. I think it's good to think about things on your own and to make some decisions for yourself."

He looked around and waited briefly for questions, but he saw everyone was eager for him to start. So Tom began. He said, "The Kumeyaay people lived in this place for a long time. Some of my archaeologist friends say that Kumeyaay have been here for more than a thousand years, but some of my people say we had always lived here. Piedras Pintadas is only one of many areas—sites, as archaeologists call them—that were occupied or used along the lower San Dieguito River. Back then, of course, the river ran where the lake is now, and some of the plants and trees were different, but the way the land looks now is pretty much the same as then."

Tom spoke thoughtfully, "If you went back in time, you wouldn't have a hard time recognizing where you were, but you would think about this place in a different way."

He went on, "Our Kumeyaay storytellers often start their stories by saying, 'A long time ago, when all the people were animals....' That's because we believe the spirits of all things lived together with the Creator when the world was very young. Back then, it was decided that for life to continue, some of the animals would have to serve as food for the others. Since that time, my people have honored those animals' sacrifice by taking their lives in a respectful manner. We have always seen ourselves as part of the natural world, not as masters of it.

"The Kumeyaay people are related to a number of other Indian groups who speak languages something like ours. Many archaeologists and Indians believe that the Kumeyaay migrated here from the Colorado River area. In fact, the Kumeyaay are closely related to several other Yuman tribes who still live along the river and in Arizona and southern Nevada. In the old days, we traded with these people and had many relatives among them. Even today, we still get together for ceremonials and to visit.

"My people knew a lot about living in dry climates, but they had to learn many new things to survive here. I think they got along real well!" He laughed, "They were probably pretty happy about all the water they found. The river and the little streams were the reason people were able to live in this valley for so long."

A hand shot up. One of the grownups asked, "Why is the lake here? Is it very old?"

Tom answered, "It's been around for a while, since the mid-1920s, but it wasn't here during the time the Kumeyaay lived here. Lake Hodges was created by damming the San Dieguito River. It's a reservoir for San Diego's drinking water.

He continued, "My people did modify the waterways here, though. Water is a sacred lifegiver. We show respect by keeping the areas near water cleared and shaded. I've been told that, in the past, my ancestors sometimes piled cobbles and other

Origin Story (continued)

When Younger Brother stroked the animal, he could tell it was not his fox. When he asked for the fox, Older Brother refused to give it to him and the two had a terrible argument. Younger Brother was so angry, he went back through the water to his home. He lives there even today—when he walks around or moves in his sleep, the earth above shakes.

Origin Story (continued)

After Younger Brother left, Older Brother was all alone and he started thinking, "I don't like so much water around me, I need some land." So he thought about it until he got an idea. He called to the red ants living below and told them to carry up some of the earth. The ants did this, piling up the earth until the water moved away.

Next Older Brother decided he needed some light. He took a piece of white clay to make the moon and threw it into the eastern sky, but it wasn't bright enough. So then he took a piece of yellow clay to make the sun and threw it into the sky near the moon, and the sun shone brightly.

rocks across streams to slow the water's course and to create ponds. These changes helped to maintain the water supply and created special places for plants, birds, and animals, like pond turtles, to live. Ponds and pools were also important for bathing and keeping things clean.

" You know," Tom said, "Some people think Indians never changed anything. They have the idea that Indians left the land just as they found it. But, like other cultures around the world, we also changed things in our environment. One way to explain it is to say we were good natural resource managers.

"I've been told, for example, that we regularly burned each area of the land and then broadcast seeds to encourage the annual plants we wanted to grow. The burn created open areas and fresh browse for the deer and other animals, as well. New plant growth kept the deer close by, so hunters didn't have to go far to find them. We experimented with many, many plants, too, always trying to move them to new places where they might grow. It takes a long time to understand how to use the resources you find around you. An important part of Kumeyaay life was finding new and better ways to use these things, not just for you and your family, but for everyone in the community.

"I thought it might be interesting to walk down the trail and see some of the plants that were here with the Kumeyaay. I'd like to tell you about some of their uses. Would you like to do that?" he asked.

Origin Story (continued)

Older Brother liked the land and the light, but he was lonely. So he took more clay and made all the animals. The animals sat around him in a circle and kept Older Brother company for awhile, but they didn't want to work, so Older Brother decided to make people from the same clay as the animals. First he made a man, and then he made a woman—then he made many people, but only Indians. The animals and the people all lived together with Older Brother. And that is what happened when the world began.

3

THE TRAIL TO THE PAST

Tom's idea pleased everyone! They all got up, and after stretching a bit, fell in behind Tom as he started down the trail. Cassie found herself near the front. She was glad because everyone else was taller than she was and she wanted to be able to see everything Tom pointed out.

As they walked, Tom stopped every so often to show them something interesting. "Here's some dodder," he would say. "It was boiled into a tea and drunk as medicine for a black widow spider's bite. Over there is some white sage, one of my favorite plants. It was used for food, for medicine, and even to purify and bless the houses. Look over here! Can you see the deer tracks? They're fresh, probably from this morning." Birds flew overhead, and Tom pointed them out. Frogs croaked in the stream next to the trail, and Tom stopped the group so they could listen. When a rabbit darted in front of them, Tom pointed out the direction he thought it would go next—and it did!

It went on and on. How could anyone know so much? Everywhere they looked there was something new to look at and learn about. The Kumeyaay had used almost everything there, and Tom seemed to know about it all!

Cassie was amazed. She had walked down the same trail almost every day and hadn't noticed any of it. Even just minutes before, when she had gathered up trash right where they were walking, she hadn't really seen. The plants and animals had always been there, but she simply hadn't looked at them. It was as if Tom was giving her a whole new world to explore with a new pair of eyes. She stopped for a moment, lagging behind, just so she could take another look around her. Scattered across the hillsides were more of the same plants Tom had been telling them about. She could see them now! She could even see some of the holes the gophers and ground squirrels had dug to hide in!

Cassie was thinking something else, too. For the first time, she felt like maybe this special place wasn't really hers after all. Her family had lived in their house for only eight years. Tom's family had lived here for centuries. She wondered how he felt about that.

By the time Cassie caught up with everyone, Tom was standing in the shade of a large, old tree. He was explaining why the tree was so important. He said, "This is a coast live oak. When Kumeyaay people lived here, there were many more of these. This is one of only a few surviving in the vicinity. Acorns were a special food item for many Indians in California, but it took time and patience to make the acorns edible. They had to be gathered, cracked, ground and reground, and they still wouldn't be ready to eat. You have to wash out the bitterness in the meal with water before it tastes good.

"The tastiest acorns are from the black oak trees up in the mountains. In the autumn, Kumeyaay people from all over went there for the acorn harvest. Each band had a specific acorn harvesting place. Some of the elders say the people from around Piedras Pintadas went up to a place near

RABBITS

Three kinds of rabbits are found around Piedras Pintadas—jackrabbit, desert cottontail, and brush rabbit. All were hunted as a very important source of food. Hunting strategies were based on careful observances of the behavioral characteristics of each of the species.

The Kumeyaay sometimes held communal rabbit hunts. Half of the group would stretch out across an area, side-by-side, with a long agave fiber net between them. The other half, armed with throwing sticks, would begin walking in a line from the opposite end, singing and scaring the rabbits from their hiding places, driving them toward the waiting net. The netted rabbits were clubbed with the throwing sticks. All participants shared in the take, with some of the meat consumed communally after the hunt. The rabbit pelts were woven into blankets or robes.

WOOD RATS

Wood rats were a favorite Kumeyaay food, valued for their excellent flavor and ease of procurement. The Kumeyaay would catch them in deadfall traps or destroy their houses and shoot them with bows and arrows as they ran out.

DEER AND PRONGHORN ANTELOPE

Deer and pronghorn antelope provided protein in the Kumeyaay diet. Deer herds were carefully managed through periodic burning of grasslands. The resulting fresh browse kept the animals within a specific territory and ensured an adequate food supply for the animals.

Less is known about Kumeyaay management of pronghorn. Hunted to extinction early in European occupation, these animals once may have been found in the upland mesa areas near Piedras Pintadas.

Mesa Grande. It was a really exciting time, because after the work was done, people had fun. There was singing and dancing and game playing, too. It was a time when everybody visited. And there was plenty to eat!"

One of the scouts wanted to know what the acorns tasted like after they had been cooked. Tom told him, "There are many different recipes. Sometimes the acorn meal is cooked into a thin cereal, other times it's made into a kind of custard. The acorn dish takes on the flavor of whatever you add to it. If you eat it with meat or flavored with dried sage or wild onions, it tastes savory. If you add fresh or dried fruit, it tastes sweet. Even though we have so many other foods, I still like my grandmother's acorn mush, ***shawii***. Once in a while she grinds up wild cherry seeds and puts them in, and that's the best!"

He went on to say, "The most important foods at Piedras Pintadas were acorns, rabbit, grains, and other seeds. Some historians who have studied Spanish records have pointed out that our people purposefully planted a now extinct grass seed and then harvested the grain."

Tom grinned, "I bet when I say 'grass' seed, you think of lawns, but these grasses were similar in size to wheat. Resource management practices like this helped to keep away hungry times here in the old days."

The group moved down the trail until they came to a rock with many holes in it. Some of the holes were deep and round, others were shallow and oval-shaped. Tom explained that the holes were used for preparing different kinds of foods. The deeper holes, called ***mortars***, were used with ***pestles*** to pound and grind acorns, as well as to grind up rodents and reptiles. The shallower holes, called ***basins***, were used for grinding smaller seeds. Sometimes portable grinding surfaces, called ***metates***, were used as well.

Tom then asked one the of grownups to put her hand down on the rock and to describe what she felt. She ran her hand around a little circular area and in a surprised voice exclaimed, "It's so smooth! It doesn't feel like the rock around it at all!"

Everyone chuckled. Then, they all wanted to feel the smooth place, too! Tom told them the smooth area was a ***slick*** and that it had been worn that way by a stone hand tool used during seed grinding. The tool that had been used was called a ***mano***.

"Why are there so many holes on this rock?" someone asked.

"Because grinding was a woman's job, and often the women liked to work together. It gave them a chance to talk and enjoy each other's company," Tom replied.

Cassie thought that sounded like fun. She remembered how much her mother liked to have Cassie's aunts in the kitchen with her when they got meals ready at holiday time. Cassie's mother always said it made the work seem like play because there was so much laughing and happy chatter. Cassie thought the Kumeyaay women had the right idea!

GRINDING TOOLS

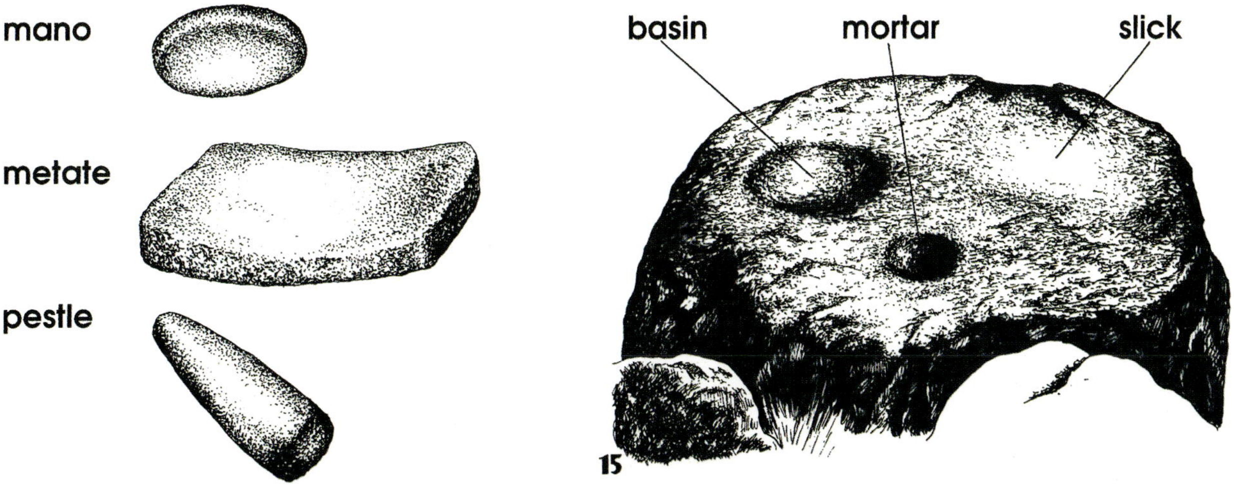

Tom continued, "Women were the providers of most of the plant foods which were an important part of the family's daily diet. The food resources in certain areas were sometimes exploited more by some families than by others, but families shared with each other and people generally had no problem obtaining permission to hunt and collect outside their own areas.

"Through the centuries, the women not only kept track of resources that belonged to their families, but discovered the secrets of making those plants grow in other places and how to use them. They knew about which plants could be eaten and which were to be avoided. Some women, and also men, were specialists in the use of plant materials as medicines. They were highly respected and always tried to pass on what they knew."

Tom added, "My grandmother knows many different plant and herbal remedies that she learned from her mother and aunts. Sometimes when I come here, I'll see a plant I know she can use and I'll take a little back for her. "

"What kinds of things did the men do?" someone asked.

Tom replied, "Lots of things, but the first that comes to mind is hunting. They used many techniques—shooting with bows and arrows, trapping in snares, using a throwing stick, communal rabbit hunts—different animals were hunted in different ways based on observation of the animal's behavior. But sometimes men also helped gather and prepare plant foods. For instance, *agave* from the desert and piñon nuts from the mountains. Burning the fields was also men's work.

"People often worked together to get jobs done. It was also a way to teach young people the skills they needed to know. Children watched how things were done and were encouraged to learn by trying the tasks for themselves. And they didn't learn just the tasks they would do as adults, they were encouraged to learn everything they needed to survive. For instance, girls learned how to make and use throwing sticks and bows and arrows, and boys learned how to prepare food."

A secret, mysterious, mischievous kind of smile slowly crept across Tom's face. It made his eyes seem to twinkle. He laughed, "In the old days, people usually didn't ask questions. They got their answers by watching what was happening and deciding for themselves. But I like asking questions—it's faster. Then, I decide for myself!"

It was getting dark. Almost two hours had passed, but no one had even noticed! The group walked back up the trail with Tom. Cassie was thinking the whole time about all the new things she'd learned that afternoon. When they'd reached the trail's end, she'd already decided for herself that she wanted to come back to help the next time. She thought she'd tell her parents and her brother and let them decide if they wanted to come along, too!

A RECIPE FOR SHAWII

1. Gather ripe acorns and let them dry in the sun for a few days. Remove caps and crack the acorns open to remove outer shells.

2. Crush acorns with a pestle in a mortar.

3. Separate out the coarser meal. Regrind until the acorn meal is the consistency of cake flour.

4. Acorn meal is high in tannic acid, which has a very bitter taste. To remove the tannic acid, put the acorn meal in a colander or loosely woven basket. Pour warm water over the meal until the water running out the bottom is clear. If you eat acorn meal without removing the tannic acid, the acorn meal will taste bad and will give you a stomachache!

5. To prepare the shawii, take some of the meal and put it in a cooking pot. Add some water until it is the consistency of oatmeal. Cook over a low heat, constantly stirring until heated through.

6. Spoon into a bowl and eat! You can add fruit if you like.

4

THE GUESSING GAME

That night at dinner, Cassie did almost all the talking! She talked about the plants she had seen. She talked about how to make acorn meal taste sweet. She talked about how beautiful everything had looked after the trash had been picked up. She talked so much and so fast that no one else, including her brother Jeffrey, could get a word in!

Finally, her father interrupted. "Cassie, slow down! I'm getting indigestion because my stomach can't keep up with you!"

With Cassie momentarily stopped, her mother asked, "Who did you say is doing this?"

Cassie began again. Only this time, she went slower. She explained that she'd been to a work party to clean up the open area and that most of the people were scouts and some of their parents. The project leader was named Tom KWA HAN, and he was an Indian—a Kumeyaay Indian—just like the people they'd learned about in school in the fourth grade. And he knew everything about the open area!

Her father looked across the table at her mother and asked, "I wonder if she means Tom Quahan, the furniture designer?"

Before her mother could answer, Cassie said, "He told us he made furniture."

"Well, I'll be darned," her father responded. "Cassie, Mr. Quahan is very well-known. He's won many awards for his furniture."

"Wow," Cassie replied. Then she began again full force. "Did you know there's a plant in the open area that will cure black widow spider bite? Did you know you can make an oven in the ground? Did you know once all the people were animals? ..."

"I guess we don't know a lot of things, Cassie," laughed her mother, interrupting her chatter. "Maybe we should go to the next work party, too. I think it would be very interesting."

****

All four McKenzies were present two weeks later for the second afternoon of cleanup. This time they met a little later in the day and the group was much larger. Some of the scouts had brought younger brothers and sisters, and some of the grownups had brought adult friends.

Tom was waiting for them all at the bottom of the trail. He had several big boxes of plastic bags at his side. He greeted each person as they arrived and introduced himself to newcomers. When it was Cassie's family's turn, her father shook Tom's hand and said how glad he was to meet him. Tom thanked him and told her father that he was pleased to see Cassie had come back and had brought so many recruits with her!

That afternoon was spent working on the far side of the ridge, in a part of the open area where Cassie and her family didn't often walk. There was another stream there that was thick with trees, and many little rock-topped hills. Cassie and her father decided to work as a team. They traded turns carrying the trash bag and joked together as they worked. Her father teased her about being afraid to

KUMEYAAY HOUSES

The Kumeyaay built different style houses for different environmental settings. Houses in the mountains were more substantial, while houses near the coast did not need to provide as much protection.

The people at Piedras Pintadas constructed their houses carefully. The positioned the houses so that sunshine could reach inside through the arched doorway. The frame poles of the house were made from young oak or sycamore branches and were set into a circle of post holes. The branches were then fastened together at the top with agave fiber cordage and other pliable limbs were added as crossbars.

Next, the frame was covered with thick bundles of deerweed or other kinds of thatch to keep off the rain. Wooden needles threaded with yucca fiber were used to tie the thatch to the frame. It took two people to finish this part of the construction.

POTTERY

Girls were instructed in pottery making by close female relatives, and fine potters were specially recognized and valued. Pottery making was a summer activity and was usually done in isolation, away from the village. To have the process witnessed by others was to invite a disastrous outcome!

The technique of Kumeyaay pottery making is known as the "paddle and anvil" method, and calls for a multi-step procedure. Pottery making could be a time consuming process with up to as many as 12 hours required in the preparation of a single piece prior to firing. A variety of cooking and storage items were created, including large and small bowls, canteens, pots, and ollas.

walk in the bushes, and she teased him about being out of shape. They also just talked.

"Dad, did you always think this place was special?" Cassie asked.

"Well, Cassie, I've always liked it, but I guess I've sort of taken it for granted for a while. It was the reason your mom and I bought the house, though. We thought it would be nice for you and Jeffrey to have a place to explore that wasn't just pavement. We hoped it would help you enjoy nature the way we do. I'm pleased that you've taken an interest in caring for the open area."

****

The work party lasted for an hour, but because there were more people this time, much more work got done. They could see how happy Tom was when they assembled for his talk. "Thank you! Thank you!" he said. He seemed to scan the group looking for someone. But when he saw that the person he was looking for wasn't there, he went on, "Last time we were together I talked about some of the plants and animals that are here. This time, I'm going to tell you about how my people lived on this land.

"If you look down to the lake you'll see where probably most of the homesites were located. A good portion of the village would be underwater now. I try to use the word 'village' carefully, because I think it implies a settlement with houses lined up along a main street! Our villages did not have streets or neat rows of houses. For one thing, the houses were spread out from each other on the lower slopes overlooking the San Dieguito River. Close, but not too close! And people didn't build their houses just anywhere. Rather, most families were related to other families in the village, and the closest relatives tried to live near each other. For example, groups of brothers often built their homes close to each other or near their parents. There was an unspoken understanding about the use of the village land. Each family was responsible for keeping the area around its house in order, and people were careful not to disturb the property maintained by others.

"Like other societies, our people chose to build their villages in attractive locations whenever possible. Here, the village had a beautiful view of the San Dieguito River. People could look out of their houses and see the valley and the mountains beyond. While they may not have lived here all year round, it was the main habitation area for Kumeyaay along this part of the river. During some times of the year, the people left their homes here to take advantage of ripening foods elsewhere. Acorns were gathered in the mountains in the autumn, and groups travelled down to the desert in the early spring to harvest agave.

"When women married they kept their own family name, and sometimes they went to live in their husband's village. But if it was anything like it is today, families stayed close and visited with each other as often as possible. Relatives were scattered through many villages, so the Kumeyaay had many

MAKING A CLAY POT THE KUMEYAAY WAY

1. Collect the clay and let it dry.
2. Crush and grind the clay. Store it for a while to let it age, then add water and mix thoroughly.
3. Take an old pot bottom and mold some of the clay against it to form a new base; remove the old bottom.
4. Roll some of the clay between your hands to make "snake-like" rope coils.
5. Press the first coil unto the pot bottom and smooth the edges with your fingers.

   Continue adding coils until the pot is the right height.
6. Holding a smooth cobble against the inside wall of the pot, press the clay against a wooden paddle held in the other hand to smooth out the ridges on the pot's surface.
7. Decorate the pot by making marks in the clay with a stick or your fingernails, or paint a design.
8. Let the pot dry.
9. With supervision, place the pot upright on a pile of dry brush, light the brush and let it burn down. Let the pot cool.
10. Dig a pit in a dry place and line with a layer of twigs followed by oak bark. Place pot upside down on the oak and then stack bark slabs over it. Light the twigs and let the fire burn down completely. Wait at least 8 hours to remove the pot.

BASKETRY

Kumeyaay women were excellent basket makers. They made both coiled and twined basketry. Baskets, especially beautifully worked, decorated examples, were prized personal possessions. Some plant species used for basketry, such as three-leaf sumac, are still found at Piedras Pintadas. Others, such as juncus and deergrass, were probably also here in the past.

CLOTHING ITEMS

Kumeyaay clothing was not particularly elaborate. Women wore two-piece skirts, front and back, of peeled and pounded willow or elder bark. The tops of the skirt pieces were woven with milkweed and other fibers to hold the bark in place and the skirt pieces were tied together at the sides when they were worn. The back piece was usually longer and thicker than the front, to provide comfortable padding when sitting on the ground or on rocks. The skirts made a wonderful swishing sound when the women walked.

travel destinations. Children belonged to their father's family and were much loved.

"There were special rules parents followed before and after a baby was born to ensure the child would grow up healthy. Parents did many things to protect their children. In the old days, babies went everywhere with the mothers. They were strapped onto cradleboards, so they would grow up with straight, strong backs, and they accompanied their mothers during all their tasks. The mothers would fashion shades to cover the babies' faces and would sometimes drape a fine soft netting over the cradleboard to keep bugs from biting. They used shredded bark as padding on the cradleboard and discarded it when it was soiled. Prehistoric disposable diapers—and biodegradable, too! New, larger cradleboards replaced the old as the baby grew.

"Everything the people needed they made for themselves or traded for. Women wove many different kinds of baskets, some very beautiful, which were used as cooking and storage vessels, plates and bowls, and even as caps. They also wove intricately knotted bags and carrying nets from fibers. Later they learned to make pottery for storing water or dry goods. They fashioned the skirts they wore from pounded willow bark. Blankets and robes were woven from ingeniously cut and twisted rabbit pelts. They even made raincoats from reeds they found along the river and sandals from the fibers of dried agave leaves.

"Men made bows from ash, mesquite, elder, or willow branches. One way to shape the bow was to dry it and then resoften the wood by burying it in wet ground and then warming it over a fire. The bow was thinned and tapered, and end notches were cut. Then, while the wood was still warm, it was gently bowed into shape and lightly strung to help retain the arc as the wood hardened. Bow strings were made of sinew, milkweed fiber, or twisted buckskin."

Tom added, "I hope you can see why the land and all the plants and animals are so important to the Kumeyaay. Our lives came from it."

One of the scouts raised his hand. "Tom, why don't the Kumeyaay live here now?"

It was very still. Tom looked down at the ground for a moment, as if he were carefully deciding about what he would say. When he finally answered the question, his voice was serious and thoughtful.

"Well, when the Spanish came here 200 years ago, they had very different ideas about how we should live. They set up a mission in San Diego to introduce us to their religion and ways. I don't know for sure if the people from Piedras Pintadas went there. If they did go, I don't know whether they went there willingly or whether they were forced to go. Some of the people may have gone to other villages farther away to escape what was happening. What I can tell you is that it was a very sad and a very hard time for the Kumeyaay. Many people died from the diseases the Spanish and other Europeans brought with them, and I think many

HUNTING IMPLEMENTS

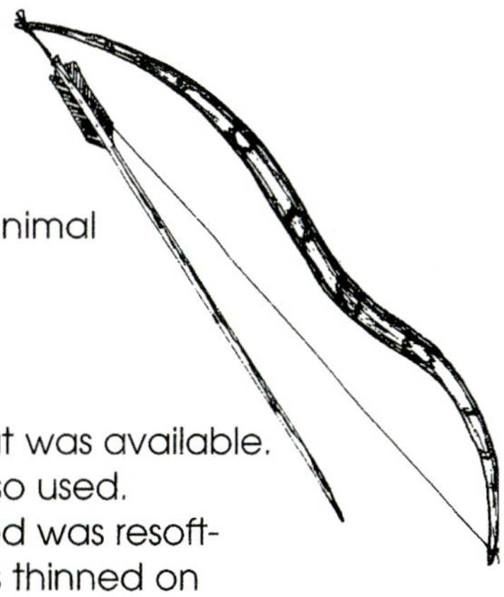

Hunting implements included wooden bows strung with deer sinew, cane arrows with wooden foreshafts which were sometimes tipped with flaked stone points, and wooden throwing sticks. Hunters also used many different types of animal traps and snares.

BOW CONSTRUCTION

Bows were constructed from various types of wood, largely depending on what was available. The best bow material was mountain ash, but elder, mesquite, and willow were also used.

Bows were usually at least five feet long. After drying a green branch, the wood was resoftened by burying it in wet ground and then warming it over a fire. The branch was thinned on one side from the midsection out, gradually tapering to the ends. Next, end notches were cut, and the still-warm wood was gently bowed into shape and lightly strung to help retain the arc as the wood hardened. Bow strings could be made of sinew, milkweed fiber, or twisted buckskin.

THROWING STICKS

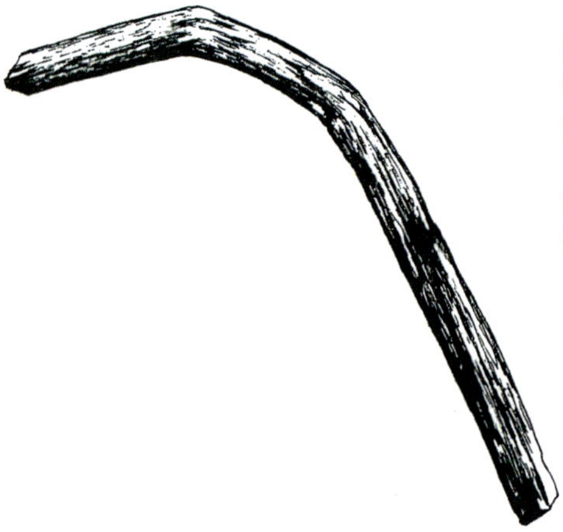

Curved sticks were used to hunt rabbits. Although shaped like boomerangs, the sticks did not return to the owner when thrown. However, they could be made to zig-zag in imitation of the running patterns of the rabbit.

Throwing sticks were made of oak, wild lilac or chokecherry. The wood was first soaked and bent and allowed to dry. It was then carved flat with a stone knife.

others died simply from the changes that came. You see, without our land, we couldn't live. When some of our people tried to resist the changes, the soldiers killed them or forced them to work at the missions.

"After a time, the missions were disbanded, but by then, of course, nothing was the same for us. The Spanish fathers at the mission had promised the Indians there that someday, when they knew enough, they would be given land to set up their own towns, but only three Indian towns were ever granted.

"One of those towns was San Pasqual. It was founded in 1835, and had a small chapel, as well as houses. The leader of this community was a man named Ponto. During his time, in 1848, the people of the village gave refuge to General Kearny's American soldiers when they fought the Mexicans at the Battle of San Pasqual, in the Mexican-American War. One of the villagers even sneaked past enemy lines and went down to San Diego to get help for the Americans.

"In 1870, President Grant set aside 92,000 acres for the San Pasqual Reservation, but the next year he rescinded his order. That's when American settlers forced the Indians to move into the hills and canyons outside San Pasqual Valley. We were left without any land at all for many years. Finally, in 1910, the government established the San Pasqual Indian Reservation, where I live."

Tom concluded with a hint of a smile, "With all the disruptions at San Pasqual, I'm sure you can understand how over the years we lost some of our cultural traditions. We've had hard times, but we're strong and we're still here! That's why Piedras Pintadas means so much to me. When I come here, I can find the past for myself. It helps me to clear my head and remember who I am, so I can live better in the present!"

Just then, out of the corner of her eye, Cassie saw a tall, dignified man approach where they were sitting. He looked a lot like Tom, but he was much older and his dark hair was cut short and sprinkled with white. The man stood quietly at a little distance and waited while Tom spoke. He held a large box in his arms.

When Tom saw the man, he smiled broadly. "Grandfather, come meet my friends!" he said. "Everyone, this is my grandfather, Eugene Quahan. I asked him to come today because I wanted him to see how well things are shaping up here. I also thought you'd probably had enough of listening to me, so we decided to share something fun."

Mr. Quahan nodded. As he stepped forward, everyone gathered around. From the box, he took a big plaid blanket and two painted wooden sticks, one white, the other black. He explained that he was going to teach them a simplified version of a very ancient game called ***peon***, or in Kumeyaay, ***oo-marp***. In the old days, he told them, this game had always been played at night. Then he asked for volunteers to make up two teams of four players each. When the players had been chosen, Mr. Quahan had one team kneel on the ground and cover their laps with the blanket. They were

GAMES

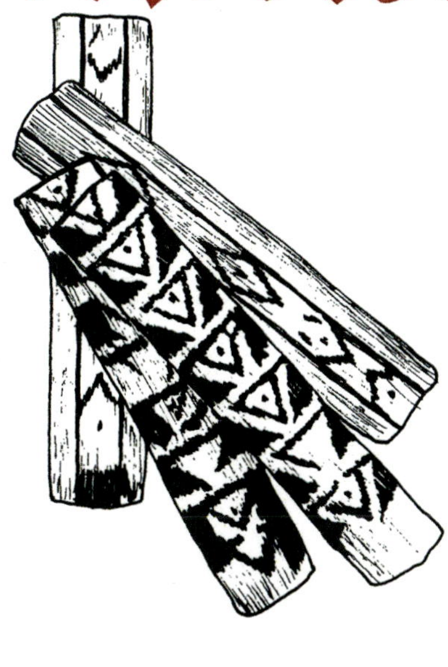

Besides peon, the Kumeyaay enjoyed many different games. The women sometimes played a game using four painted wooden dice. Women and girls also played a string figure game, something like cat's cradle. The figures they made were named after some of the characters and elements of Kumeyaay mythology—Coyote's nose, Wild Cat's head, and the Milky Way.

Men liked to play a hoop and stick game. In one version, the player would roll a hoop and try to throw a stick through it while it was moving. Another way the game was played was to try to make the hoop fall over on the pole's marked tip in order to score.

instructed to put their hands under the blanket, and he gave them the two sticks. The sticks, he said, were to be passed back and forth under the blanket while they sang a song. When the song ended, they were to stop. The object of the game was for the opposite team to guess together who had the white stick. After they had made their guess, the players were to drop the blanket and show who really held the stick. The onlookers were to encourage their team by joining in with the singing and helping to distract the guessers from watching what was happening under the blanket.

For the rest of the afternoon, they played peon. Mr. Quahan showed the teams how to sway back and forth to disguise their hand motions and he kept score for them with another set of sticks he had brought along. They sang all the camp songs they knew, and they laughed as the guesses were made. The teams were changed often, so everyone got a chance to play.

Cassie loved playing the game. But the very best round was when Mr. Quahan came and sat next to her on her team. Cassie's brother Jeffrey was on the opposite side, and he guessed the white stick was in Mr. Quahan's hand. But when the blanket was dropped, everyone saw that Cassie had it. Mr. Quahan leaned over and whispered, "Good job!"

CRADLEBOARDS

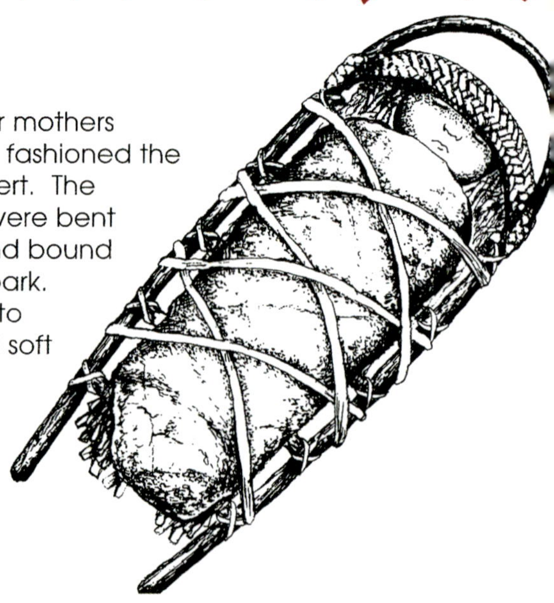

Strapped onto cradleboards, babies accompanied their mothers everywhere for the first years of their lives. Women typically fashioned the carrier frames from mesquite branches gathered in the desert. The branches were softened over a fire until pliable, and then were bent into a hairpin shape. Short lengths of mesquite were cut and bound between the sides of the frame with strips of desert cedar bark.

Curved wicker basketry shades were sometimes added to cradleboards to protect the baby from the sun's glare, and soft pillow pads of shredded desert cedar bark were placed to cushion the baby's head.

5
A VISIT WITH AN ARCHAEOLOGIST

There were more work parties. Sometimes Cassie's whole family went and other times Cassie went by herself or took her best friends Susan and Tricia with her. Each time, Tom rewarded their efforts by telling them something new about the open area or about the way the Kumeyaay had lived. It was always fun.

One special afternoon when the group had gathered to work, Cassie saw Tom standing with a large, burly man. From the way they were joking together, she knew they were friends. Then Tom told them he had a surprise. No work today, he said. Instead of picking up trash, he told them he thought a treat was in order. He had invited Chris Markham, an archaeologist who taught at the university, to show them a skill from the past.

Dr. Markham stepped forward and set down a folding stool. From a heavy-looking knapsack, he took out a plastic tarp, which he laid out in front of the stool, a number of stones, some of which were whole, others which were broken, a large piece of leather, and some large and small pieces of antler. He put the stones and the pieces of antler on the tarp and sat down on the stool with the leather pad on his lap.

"I know that Tom has been telling you about how the Kumeyaay people lived at Piedras Pintadas, so this afternoon I'm going to show you how some of the tools they used were made. I've been learning stone toolmaking for a long time and I want you to remember this isn't something you should try unless you're with someone who can guide you." He held up his hand to show them the bandages he wore on two fingers!

He pulled out a pair of leather gloves and a pair of goggles from his jacket pocket and put them on. Then he picked up one of the rocks in front of him and held it up in his fist so they could see it.

"I think that one of the greatest achievements humans ever made happened over 2 million years ago when someone looked at a round rock and realized that inside was a sharp edge." He turned the rock in his hand to reveal that one side of it had been worked away to form a cutting edge.

Adjusting the leather pad on his lap, Dr. Markham picked up another fist-sized rock and struck it several times against the edge of the round rock he held. "This is called percussion flaking. What I'm doing is striking a downward blow to detach large pieces of rock. The rock that strikes the other is called a ***hammerstone***, and the rock that's being struck is called a ***core***. The piece that comes off is called a ***flake***. If I turn the flake over, on the back is a circular round raised area called the ***bulb of percussion***. It's created by the force of the blow to the core.

"When the flake detaches from the core, it leaves a depressed place called a ***flake scar*** that marks the place where the flake came off. Occasionally when I'm working in the field, I come across flakes near a core and I can fit the flakes back in by matching the bulbs to the scars. Bulbs and scars are important to archaeologists because

ARROWHEADS

Kumeyaay arrowheads were made from quartz, metavolcanics, and sometimes obsidian. They are small in size and triangularly shaped, with a concave base. Some of the points were created with great care and precision, while others were shaped just enough to be functional. The carefully worked points may have ritual significance rather than a utilitarian function.

STONE TOOLS

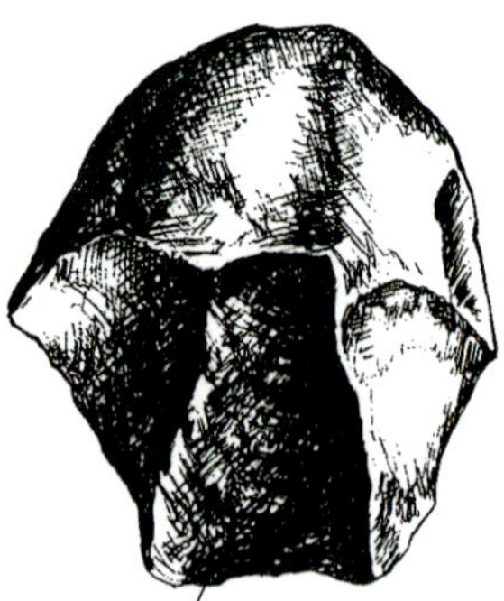

A Core
A Flake Scar

A Flake
A Bulb of Percussion

they tell us people were at work. Nature also produces bulbs and scars—rocks tumble against each other in streams or press against each other deep in the earth—but nature works randomly. If we see a pattern of scars, for instance, then we know what we are looking at is manmade."

Dr. Markham carefully passed around the flakes and core so everyone had a chance to see and feel what he had described. Next, he picked up one of the flakes. "This can be used as a tool," he said. "In fact, when I passed it around before, I was careful not to have anyone touch the edges because they're very sharp." To demonstrate this, he picked up a corner of his leather pad and cut off a small piece of it with the flake.

"This one flake is all you would need to skin a rabbit. And you probably would only need one or two to skin a deer. Sharp flakes are effective cutting tools, some are even better than steel knife blades." Everyone exclaimed at that.

Tom had been standing behind the others while Dr. Markham was talking. He laughingly called out a challenge, "O.K., Chris, it's time to show what you can really do! Make an arrowhead for us!"

Dr. Markham flashed an enormous smile. "I was hoping you'd ask me to do that. I've been saving the best for last!" He reached into his knapsack and took out a fist-sized chunk of shiny black obsidian.

"Obsidian is volcanic glass. Each volcano has a unique chemical composition, so if we analyze the elements we find in an obsidian sample, we can determine the obsidian's source. This piece of obsidian came from a volcano in a place called Obsidian Butte, near the Salton Sea."

He slowly turned the obsidian in his hand, looking carefully to find a starting place. When he found the place he liked, he struck the obsidian several times with a small hammerstone and then selected one of the flakes. He explained he was going to first shape the flake into a ***blank***, and then he was going to make it into the finished arrowhead. When he had finished the blank, he held the piece up to show its oval shape.

Next, Dr. Markham picked up a piece of antler. Putting his other hand through an opening in the leather pad, he positioned the blank carefully in his palm and pressed the tip of the antler against the edge of the blank in a downward fashion. A short ribbon of obsidian popped off the bottom. He repeated this again and again, down one side and up the other. Then he turned the piece over and repeated the process.

"This is the easy part," Dr. Markham told them, as he showed them how the arrowhead now looked. "It gets trickier. In the next step, I have to thin the base, then I have to carefully work the tip to make it sharp, and then the last step is to punch out little crescent-shaped flakes on the sides to make two notches. I have to really concentrate now on what I'm doing, so I don't accidently break the arrowhead."

It grew very quiet. They all watched anxiously as the toolmaker worked. He stopped to show his progress as each step was completed, until, at last,

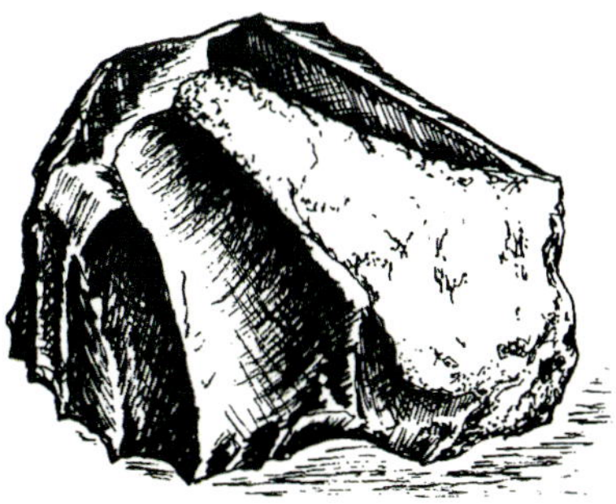

A Domed Scraper
(used to work wood, hides, or fibers)

A Biface
(used as a cutting implement)

he triumphantly held up the finished arrowhead. Everyone applauded!

Dr. Markham passed the arrowhead around for closer inspection. It was beautiful! When it reached Cassie she could see a kind of wavy pattern that had been created as Dr. Markham had pressed off all the tiny flakes. He had worked the arrowhead so finely that she could almost see through it when she held it up against the sun. The notches had been shaped so well that the tip of her little finger barely fit into them and the top of the arrowhead was indeed sharp and perfectly positioned.

Tom's beaming face showed he was very proud of his friend. And he beamed even more when Dr. Markham placed the arrowhead in his hand and asked him to keep it safe.

Archaeologists call the two types of small arrowheads made by the Kumeyaay the Cottonwood point and the Desert Side-Notched point.

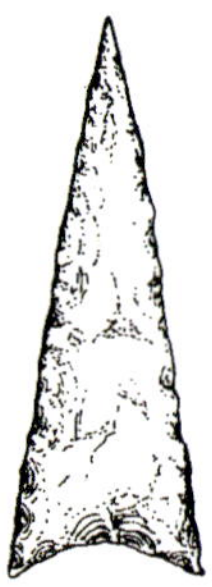

A Cottonwood Point

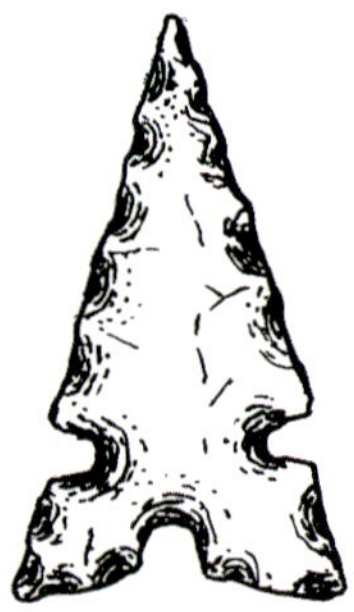

A Desert Side-Notched Point

6

THE PAINTED ROCKS

A few Saturdays afterward, Cassie was upstairs cleaning her bedroom, something she really didn't like to do. Saturday at the McKenzies' was usually a do-something-you-didn't-like-to-do-so-you-could-do-something-fun-on-Sunday day. Ordinarily everybody pitched in to get the laundry and housework done, but today was an exception. Her father had gone into the office to finish a project and her brother had gone to friend's house to work on a school report. Cassie and her mother were alone in the house. For a while, she could hear her mother running the vacuum cleaner downstairs, then the noise stopped.

Cassie thought her room would be more cheerful with the curtains out of the way. As she pushed them aside to let in the light, she looked out the window and saw Tom standing on a hillside. He was staring down at the rocks that lined the stream below the hill. She called to her mother to come and look.

In a puzzled voice, Cassie's mother asked, "There wasn't supposed to be a work party today, was there?" Then she said, "Maybe Tom needs help. Let's go see what's going on." The two grabbed their sweaters, ran down the stairs and out the back door.

When they got to the base of the hill, they could see something wasn't right. Tom was pacing back and forth looking sad and angry at the same time. Cassie started to go toward him, but her mother held her back.

"This looks private to me, Cassie. I don't think we should intrude. Let's wait here and see what happens." She put her arm around Cassie's shoulder and they sat on the ground and waited quietly. They saw Tom climb down to the rocks with a silvery-colored plant in his hand. Cassie tried to remember from Tom's talk which one it was—sage, she thought. Then they heard a soft sort of singing like sometimes Cassie heard in church. It sounded important—and very personal. She was glad her mother had made them stop.

After a while, Tom came back up the hill. His head was down, but he didn't seem quite so angry. When he saw them, he walked over and said "Hello," but there was something painful in his greeting.

"When I came out here this morning, I discovered that someone has painted graffiti all over the rocks along the stream. The paint is everywhere," he said. "I was just walking back to my car to get some rags to see if I could wash it off."

With a look of horror on her face Cassie's mother said, "Oh, Tom, how terrible! We've got rags and soap and buckets in the garage. We'll help you." They took off and were back in no time at all.

All morning long, the three clambered over the rocks, washing and scrubbing. Luckily, the paint came off, but it had to be rubbed hard. The surface of the rocks was worn smooth in some places. The paint came off easier on the smooth places. It was much harder to get the paint off the rough surfaces. Cassie rubbed until her arms ached.

ROCK ART AT PIEDRAS PINTADAS

Piedras Pintadas is set apart from most other archaeological sites by its remarkable rock art. Nine rock art panels are found here, all painted on the faces of freestanding granitic boulders. Examples of painted rock art are called ***pictographs***. Sometimes rock art designs are pecked into the rock surface. Examples of this type of rock art are called ***petroglyphs***.

Rock Art Design from Piedras Pintadas

Rock Art Designs from Piedras Pintadas

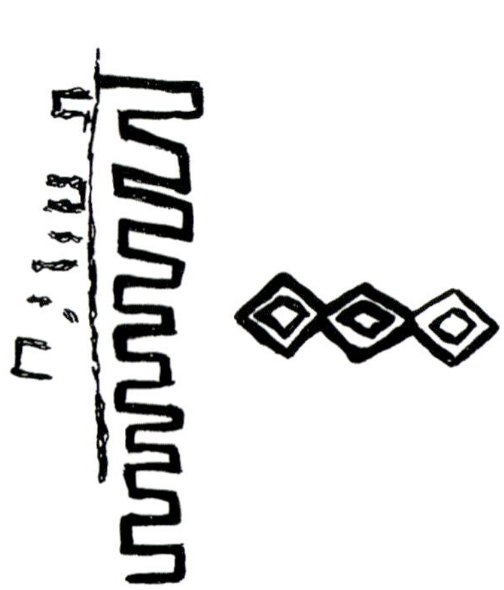

The Piedras Pintadas rock art is painted in what anthropologists call the "Rancho Bernardo Style". The most characteristic motif is a maze-like design of parallel lines joined at right angles. Other motifs include fret patterns, diamonds and diamond chains, zigzag lines, chevrons, and cross-hatching. The red paint used to create the designs was made from iron oxide mixed with a natural binding material, possibly seed oils or bird egg. The black paint probably was made from manganese dioxide, a graphite-like substance.

While she worked, Cassie thought about the long ago time when the Kumeyaay were there. About how important the water was, and how lovingly it had been cared for. She wondered if any Kumeyaay children had ever splashed in the stream. For a moment in her mind, she could see them playing, and she imagined their happy squeals. In any event, she was sure nothing so disrespectful would ever have occurred. She felt angry, and ashamed, too, because she knew the graffiti hadn't been painted by any Indian. She kept waiting for Tom to say something about it, but he never did.

Finally, when they were almost through, Cassie's mother went back up to the house and brought back some sandwiches, drinks, and fruit. The three climbed up the hill and sat under a large sumac bush where they ate their lunch. They listened to the sound of the water flowing below them and each thought how beautiful it was. Nobody said very much. They were too hot and tired, and somehow Cassie knew talking wasn't right.

At last, Cassie's mother softly apologized to Tom. "I'm sorry this happened. Not just because this place is important to you, but because it should be important to everyone."

Tom quietly thanked them both for their help and explained that if it ever happened again to be sure to call him, so he could be there.

Cassie waited for Tom to say something more to her mother. But he didn't respond immediately. He seemed to be thinking about something very carefully. Then he said, "I think you need to understand why I'd like you to call."

Tom stood up and asked them to follow him up higher on the hill. When he got to a large boulder, he pushed aside a sumac bush that had grown next to it and pointed to a place on the rock.

Cassie heard her mother draw in a deep breath of surprise and delight. She followed Tom's finger to where he was pointing and there, outlined in red was a design painted on the rock! It was almost as tall as she was and much wider, and it looked like a puzzle maze. The lines of the design were parallel to each other and they seemed to dance with energy.

"This is why the site is called Piedras Pintadas," he said. "It means 'painted rocks' in Spanish. I was planning to show it to the scouts at our next meeting, but I thought you deserved to see it first. I'd like to show you some of the other paintings."

They went on to several more boulders. Each was a canvas for more rock art. Besides the maze pattern, Cassie saw diamonds and circles that seemed to form chains. There were "V"-shapes nested one on top of another and zigzag lines, too. Each painting was different from all the others, but there seemed to be a common thread that tied them all together. All the paintings were done in red, except for one that had what looked like black "X"s in the middle.

Some of the paintings were surrounded by large sumacs. If you didn't know where to look for the drawings, you wouldn't see them. It was as if the bushes had grown up around the rocks to protect

The Piedras Pintadas rock art is thought to have been painted about 500 years ago. Certain aspects of the art support the idea that some of the paintings may be the creation of a single artist—lines are uniform in width and the designs are well-controlled. If not the work of an individual, it has been suggested the rock art style may have been "owned" by a family or clan, with patterns reproduced over a period of time by members of the group.

Rock Art Designs from Piedras Pintadas

them. Other boulders, though, stood open and exposed. From them, Cassie could easily see the back of her house. The paintings had always been there, she just hadn't known.

Tom explained, "One of my friends at the Museum of Man has told me he thinks the paintings were done about 500 years ago. They may represent the work of a single artist or perhaps artists from one family that owned the designs. My friend thinks the style probably started in the desert and was brought to this area. There are similar rock art panels found elsewhere, but the greatest number and the best examples are found in Rancho Bernardo."

With a concerned look Cassie's mother asked, "Do many people know about the rock art?"

Tom answered, "Probably too many. Most of the people who do know are respectful. They come to admire the paintings and leave them alone. So far, nothing has happened to them." He fell silent, and Cassie knew he was thinking about how close the graffiti had come to the hill. She understood now why Tom had been so angry and upset. "What can we do to protect the paintings?" Cassie's mother wanted to know. "Can't we do something to make sure people don't harm them?"

Tom's face brightened, "A big part of the worry is going to go away soon. The site will be part of the San Dieguito River Park, and there are plans to take care of the rock art, as well as provide visitors with information about how things used to be here. Our tribal council has been working with the Park planners and other people in the community for a long time and I think the outcome will be very good," he said.

He thought for a moment and added, "You could help though by watching over the site." He caught Cassie's eye. "I bet you can see all over the valley from your house!"

"That's an excellent idea," Cassie's mother said. "I'm sure many of our neighbors would want to do the same. We all love walking here and I think if they knew what's really here, they'd love it even more. Maybe we could start a neighborhood watch program."

Cassie could tell Tom was pleased. He was smiling to himself. They stayed a little longer looking at the rock art, but finally, it was time to leave.

Heading back, the three walked together and started to say their goodbyes. Right before the trail split, one way going to Tom's car and the other going up to Cassie's house, Cassie thought of something very important she needed to know. She waited until her mother had gone on ahead a little and then she summoned up the courage to ask. "Tom, what does the rock art mean?" she asked.

He slowly smiled one of those secret, mysterious, mischievous smiles, and replied, "Well, I've decided what it means to me, Cassie, but I think I'll let you decide for yourself what it means to you!" And he winked at her.

The End

No one besides the Kumeyaay knows for sure what the rock art means. But elsewhere in the world, rock art has been linked to the activities of shamans (religious specialists), astronomical observations, ritual stories, and ***rites of passage***.

STEWARDSHIP

Everywhere around us on public lands are important resources, both natural and cultural, that belong to us all. Such resources might include an ancient archaeological site or perhaps a fragile natural habitat that is home to special birds or animals. Some of these resources may be protected by public agencies, but many others are vulnerable.

Stewardship is the idea that as citizens of a community we are all responsible for these resources. It means that their care and well-being is up to us, and that as responsible citizens, we must see that no harm comes to them so that they can survive for future generations to enjoy.

Stewardship is also about respect—respect for nature and respect for other people's beliefs and values, no matter how different from our own they may be. When we accept our role as stewards, we agree to work together with others to protect the resources we value. In return, we may be given the gift of seeing the world through another person's or culture's perspective or knowing that with our help, a natural environment has been preserved or restored. Practicing stewardship makes our lives richer.

Maybe you know about a resource that needs your attention. Here are a few ways to become its steward:

- Find a group that works to protect a resource. Scout troops, for example, often take on special areas as a project. Museums and schools are other places to find interested groups. If you can't find an existing group, start one yourself.
- Always treat the resource with respect and at a distance. Look, but don't touch, unless you know for sure it's allowed.
- Keep the area around a resource clean! Don't litter, and pick up trash you come across, even if it isn't yours. This is another way to show respect.
- Keep an eye on things! If you see evidence of vandalism, report it.
- Share what you know about the resource with others. Help others to appreciate it the way you do!

GLOSSARY

Agave An important desert plant that provided the Kumeyaay with food and fiber.

Anthropology The study of man.

Archaeology The study of past cultures.

Basin A shallow oval depression created in a bedrock milling station; used for grinding food.

Blank A roughly shaped tool form.

Bulb of Percussion The circular raised area on the back of a flake created by the force of the blow that detached it from the core.

Core A rock from which flakes are struck or pressed off.

Flake The piece of rock struck or pressed from a core.

Flake Scar The depression on the core marking where the flake detached.

Hammerstone A rock used to strike flakes from a core.

Mano A handheld grinding tool.

Metate A flat grinding surface. Some metates were portable.

Mortar A deep grinding hole.

Peon *(Oo-marp)* An ancient Kumeyaay ceremonial gambling game.

Pestle An oblong pounding tool used to crush acorns and other foods.

Petroglyph A rock art design which is pecked into the rock.

Pictograph A rock art design which is painted onto the rock.

Rite of Passage A ceremony marking one's transition from one stage in life to another. In Kumeyaay culture, both boys and girls celebrated the transition from childhood to adulthood wih instructional events and rituals.

Shawii *(Sha-wee)* Kumeyaay mush or custard made from acorn meal.

Slick A smooth surface created for grinding seeds.

SUGGESTED READING AND REFERENCE MATERIAL

Anza-Borrego A to Z: People, Places, and Things — Diana Lindsay

This comprehensive encyclopedia includes information regarding early Native American history and place names of the greater desert region.

Baja California Plant Field Guide, 3rd ed. — J. Rebman & N. Roberts

Over 750 plant species are describeds in detail, including the Indian use of plants.

Baja Legends: Historic Characters, Events, and Locations — Greg Niemann

A wonderful compilation of information about Baja California that includes information about the indigenous people of the peninsula.

Camino Real and Missions of Baja California Peninsula — Miguel Leon-Portilla

A bilingual account of the missions of Baja California that includes information about the native peoples of the peninsula.

Cave Paintings of Baja California — Harry W. Crosby

This full-color account documents a world-class archaeological region in remote central Baja California.

Delfino Cuero: Her Autobiography, An Account of Her Last Years and her Ethnobotanic Contributions — Delfino Cuero

Florence Shipek interviewed Delfino Cuero and transcribed this autobiography to help Delfino prove she was born and raised in the United States.

Desert Legends & Lore of CA's Colorado and Mojave Deserts — Choral Pepper

Indian myths are included in his compilation of stories, legends and fables of the California lower desert areas.

Dictionary of Mesa Grande Diegueño — Ted Couro & Christina Hutcheson

This is the first dictionary of Yuman Indian language. It introduces the world of words, sounds and ideas of a still vital culture of southern California.

Dreamers of the Colorado: Mojave Indians, Part I — F. O'Neil & P. Wittmer, eds.

A selection of readings describe the Mojave land and religion.

Dreamers of the Colorado: Mojave Indians, Part II — F. O'Neil & P. Wittmer, eds.

A selection of readings describe the Mojave culture and arts.

Earth Pigments & Paint of the California Indians — Paul D. Campbell

Great scholarship is used in describing the technology and technique for creating the paints needed for Native American rock art in California.

Forgotten Artist: Indians of Anza-Borrego and Their Rock Art — Manfred Knaak

Rock Art sites of the Cahuilla and Kumeyaay Indians of this desert area are featured in this visually stunning book.

Fry Bread Man — Rikki Pierce

In this fable a Fry Bread man romps through a Hopi Indian Village.

Grass Games and Moon Races — Jeannine Gendar

California Indian games and toys are described through personal accounts.

Indians of the Oaks — Mellicent H. Lee

Two tales that help to describe the early life of the Kumeyaay from a child's perspective.

Jackpot Trail: Indian Gaming in Southern California — D. Valley & D. Lindsay

The history of the gaming tribal bands is reviewed along with contemporary descriptions of the casinos.

Just before Sunset — Lora Cline

Describes the life of the Kwaaymi or Mountain Kumeyaay – their culture, lifeways, and survival skills.

Marshal South and the Ghost Mountain Chronicles — Diana Lindsay, ed.

Many of South's monthly articles written for Desert Magazine from 1939-1948 contain references to Indian use of plants.

My Ancestors' Village — Roberta Labastida

The traditional ways of the Kumeyaay Indians are described by a young girl.

Native Ways: California Native Indian Stories — Malcolm Margolin

Various aspects of traditional and contemporary CA Indian life are described.

Nicio and Cedar Fire — Gina Aguilera

A modern fable for young people, this is the richly illustrated tale of a Native American fireman who fights to save his home from San Diego's 2003 devastating forest fire, dubbed the Cedar Fire. In the story he reminisces about his family and childhood; dreams about pre-Columbian Mesoamerican gods; and is ultimately saved by a Thunderbird.

Painted Rocks Ruth. Alter

A young girl acts as a guide through this important archaeological site giving information about how the Kumeyaay lived their daily lives.

Palm Springs Legends: Creation of a Desert Oasis Greg Niemann

From the Land of the Cahuilla to the Legacy of Indian Canyons, 50 fascinating vignettes portray this storied land.

Predicting the Past: An Introduction to Anthropological Archaeology David H. Thomas

Describes how anthropologists are able to describe the past through evidence left by early cultures.

Ramona Helen Hunt Jackson

A huge popular and critical success when it was first published in 1884, Ramona is set among the California Spanish missions and tells the story of the young mixed-blood heroine, Ramona, and her Native American lover Alessandro, as they flee from the brutal violence of white settlers.

Rock Art of the Grand Canyon Region D. Christensen, J. Dickey, S. Freers

Details and beautiful photographs document over 500 rock art sites of the Grand Canyon region in this lavishly illustrated book.

San Diego: California's Cornerstone Iris Engstrand

The first chapters delve into the early history of the Native Americans of San Diego.

San Diego Legends Jack Innis

Includes the many Kumeyaay legends originally gathered by Melicent Lee.

Strangers in a Stolen Land: History of Indians in San Diego Co Richard Carrico

Details about the early treatment of Native Americans and their struggle to obtain rights to their own land.

Sugar Bear Story E. Ygnacio-DeSoto

A Chumash tale about how to be a good host.

Survival Skills of Native California Paul Campbell

A "how to" manual of the skills needed to hunt, gather, and prepare food and to build shelters and other things needed in life.

Way We Lived: California Indian Stories Malcolm Margolin

A collection of stories, love songs, chants, and more from the native people of California.